FAMILY AS A BUSINESS

and

Practical Life Advice

2nd Edition

Arvind K. Garg
B.Sc. (Engineering), MBA

Make your life and family a success!

TABLE OF CONTENTS

Acknowledgments 7
Preface 9

PART I - FAMILY AS A BUSINESS

Chapter 1 Introduction.. 15
    1.01 Why a Family Is a Business 15
    1.02 What Is a Family Board 17
Chapter 2 Financial Planning 19
    2.01 What Is In a Budget? 19
    2.02 Avoid Debt Traps 20
    2.03 Elements of Cashflow 21
    2.04 How to Calculate Net Worth 24
    2.05 Is Insurance Important? * 27
    2.06 Credit cards and fees * 31
    2.07 Planning for emergencies * 33
    2.08 Having Financial Goals 35
Chapter 3 Investing 37
    3.01 Investment Goals 37
    3.02 What are Investment Criteria 38
    3.03 Time Value of Money 40
    3.04 Investing vs. Gambling 43
    3.05 Buying a House and/or Car * 45
    3.06 Types of Bank Accounts * 48
    3.07 Loans and interest * 49
    3.08 Summary Points 54
Chapter 4 Decision Making 57
    4.01 What is Decision Analysis 57
    4.02 Decision Tree Basics 58
    4.03 Expected Monetary Value 61
    4.04 Careful of Decision Bias 65

PART II - PRACTICAL LIFE ADVICE

Chapter 5 Code of Conduct.. 69
    5.01 Being on Time 69
    5.02 Children 70
    5.03 Work Life Balance * 73
    5.04 Life Rules & Principles... 75
    5.05 What Are Your Personal Values........................... 78
    5.06 Other Tips 79
Chapter 6 Sensitive Topics... 81
    6.01 Importance of Health 81
    6.02 How Does Religion Fit 82
    6.03 Death & Wills 85
Chapter 7 What Schools Don't Teach... 87
Chapter 8 Quotes... 93
Chapter 9 Closing Remarks 97

* *Sections marked with an asterisk are new or updated for 2nd edition*

ACKNOWLEDGMENTS

We have the benefit of coming across so many wonderful people throughout our life who are filled with knowledge, advice, wisdom, and affection. Unfortunately, we get so busy in our own lives that we forget to take notice and, more importantly, learn from them through their successes or their failures.

This book is a tribute to all those who have been part of my life. I have gained so much from all of you. You have enriched my life in many ways to make it more enjoyable. Has my life been perfect? No, but I don't think anyone's life is. How we look at life is an attitude. In principle, we all have the basic necessities. It's our thinking that makes us feel life should be better.

Most of all, I would like to dedicate this book to my family. I have a wife and three children (two daughters and one son). They are my pride, joy, and they have patiently supported me in all challenges. Each of them is successful in their own endeavors while maintaining family values. I am proud of their achievements. No matter how or where life has taken us around the world, they have stood together and supported family decisions with full dedication, always willing to sacrifice themselves for each other. A father-husband could not have asked for more.

Finally, I (only) am responsible for any errors and omissions in this book.

Arvind Garg

PREFACE

The ideas in this book started out as simple rules of thumb for my children to use in their adult future. After becoming adults and using the lessons they learned growing up, they realized the true value of the lessons. They asked me to write down my thoughts and views on life so they could follow them with their future families and kids, believing they should be shared with others. When I started to do this, more things came to mind which I thought would be beneficial to know and remember. Later, when I shared my views with them and other friends, everyone kept saying "Arvind, you should write a book." They found my ideas and approaches simple, practical, and logical. After everyone's insistence, I decided to put my wisdom on paper. If this book makes others' lives easier or better, my mission is accomplished.

The items presented in this book helped my family get to where we are today. Perhaps some background on me may help set the scene on why this book is important to any family.

I was born in India and migrated to the U.S. when I was three. My father enjoyed moving, so I grew up living in four different states, nine houses, and attended eight schools by the time I graduated high school at age fifteen. With the change that constantly happened in my life, I never had an emotional attachment to a location or house. The stability in life was family, as that was constant.

I graduated with my B.Sc. in Engineering at nineteen. While working, I obtained an MBA nine years later. My career lasted more than thirty years working for three multi-national corporations in the energy industry. Through my career, my family and I lived and worked in five countries (USA, Netherlands, Oman, UAE,

Singapore) and were able to travel to more than 35 countries – personally and professionally.

During my career, I met many professionals who diligently worked to make their companies successful for the future. This is the priority of all employees – as it was for me. Everyone puts in a lot of effort to make the success happen: working overtime, working from home, sacrificing personal enjoyment for work commitments, etc. I respect and applaud all who do this, provided it fits their long-term goals.

But then, I got thinking. For the effort we put in to make our employers successful (using financial statements to manage company performance, using business tools to make decisions, etc.), why can't we do the same thing with our families? Why can't we treat our family as a company and take similar measures to be successful? Afterall, if your family is happy and successful, you will perform better on the job.

A family entity is no different than a business - there are personal goals, financial goals, team goals, future growth, security, etc. So, why can't we use the same methods for a family as we do with a business? Hence, the title "Family as a Business".

This book is not about where to invest. There are a lot of other ways to learn about that. This book is based on items that relate a business to a family. It also encompasses many other life lessons. I realize not all topics will apply to everyone, as all families are different. Hence, the table of contents provides an easy guide that you can refer to according to your individual needs.

All the material in this book is generic and has been gathered from my life experiences and advice people have sent me, tools used in companies, and other various tidbits. Whenever I heard or saw something I felt could be relevant, I would make a note of it. I personally have used all the topics referenced in this book. They have worked well for me which is why I present them here. However, all numbers in the diagrams or examples represented are shown for illustrative purposes only.

By applying the tools mentioned in this book, I was (fortunately) able to resign at 53. I am now semi-retired and run my own consulting company. The main focus of my work currently revolves around providing business and commercial training to companies. I am also an adjunct professor for an executive MBA program in the U.S.

This book touches many topics, some more sensitive than others. While reading it, I hope you keep an open mind to look at things differently. Remember that what is presented here are only generic views. The guidance is based on rationale and logic, not emotion. The minute you bring in words such as "I want", "I feel", or "I believe", it is hard to argue these with logic. Change the word 'want' to 'need' and you have a very different discussion. There is no intent to single out any person, company, or group of people.

Some items may appear to be common sense – that's okay! Unfortunately, we tend to forget the basic common-sense items and concentrate on the more difficult ones. That's why many of the chapters are short and easy to understand. My goal is that readers (of all ages) use this book as a basic reference which will help them talk about the issues presented.

I am sure there are 'experts' who have a different approach or have their own better view on a topic. That's fine and I encourage you to take their input. It is always better to get many different opinions, rank them, but make the final decision yourself. If you have a method that works for you and gets your family to where you want, more power to you. I share the methods in this book because it worked for us and others I know.

I was happy that people enjoyed reading the first edition and appreciated the excellent feedback provided on possible additions. I have done my best to incorporate that feedback in this second edition.

As before, most of this book, especially specific chapters, can be applied to every family and I sincerely hope that you use the relevant parts to make a better future for your entity, whatever that may be. Good luck!

PART I

FAMILY AS A BUSINESS

Chapter 1 INTRODUCTION

1.01   Why a Family Is a Business

After many years in my career, I started looking at the tools, decisions, and methods that companies use to decide what to do next in their portfolio. It then occurred to me, 'Why can't I apply those same concepts to my family?' So, I started doing just that.

The more I delved into it, the more I realized how many similarities there are between planning for family and company success:
- Entity goals (Family/company)
- Financial goals
- Team goals
- Require future growth
- Want some type of security to protect what they have
- Annual and future cashflow concerns
- Need to invest and have investment criteria
- Maintain a respectable net worth that grows for sustainability
- Don't want to retire broke (or become liquidated)

When I teach professionals, one question I ask the class is:
If there was a company who earned (net) $1bln every year for 20 years (hence $20bln), but then after 20 years had nothing to show for it (balance sheet & net worth zero), what would you say about that company?

This would result in the usual responses of 'Poorly managed company', 'Did not plan for the future', 'Costs were not kept under control', 'Did not track what they were doing', 'Would not want to be part of a company like that', etc.

To which I would then ask: *Let's assume that on average each of you earn X (say $75K) per year for 20 years (20X = $1.5mln earnings), but also have nothing to show for it. How are you better than the company? (Note the absolute number is not important, it's the principle).*

Normally, I would get silence. Most had never thought about their life that way, but realized it is a fair question and they are not prepared for the result. Then there are those who try to defend their position with...
- 'We have a lot of expenses' (sorry, so do companies)
- 'We have to support a family' (sorry, a company has to pay employees)
- My personal favorite 'We invested all our money in our kids'. This may appear noble, but what happens after the kids leave home? Who will support you then? Will you be able to retire with the lifestyle you expect? If you believe your kids will support you in your retirement, then I agree they were an investment. If not, then they are also an expense which has to be managed.

Let me be clear, kids are not a wrong expense. Children are special and bring joy to one's life – I have three wonderful kids and enjoyed watching them grow, develop, and mature. Yes, we should spend on them to give them their own experiences. But children are not an excuse to not have a financial future for yourself, to live paycheck to paycheck, and to doubt if you will be able to comfortably retire the way you want.

The summary lesson to the above example is:
If you can't manage your own money properly, what qualifies you to decide on spending your company's money?

Yet we continue to freely spend company money without managing our own properly.

1.02   What Is a Family Board

As every company has a board (directors and shareholders), a family also has a board. Normally, the parents are the board of directors and the children are shareholders. If one wants, extended family members can be considered stakeholders. It is the role of the board to make sure the company entity operates properly and works together to make the entity successful. All stakeholders should be considered in decisions when needed. Otherwise, it is very easy for the entity to suffer.

Likewise, there needs to be a decision-making process for the entity. What priorities should the family focus on for the next year? What are issues that could affect the entity? Making proper decisions with the correct rationale is important for businesses and families. There is more on decision making in Chapter 4.

We (my family) routinely had 'family board meetings' where we would discuss the important issues that would affect the family for the upcoming few months. Obviously, the meeting content varied depending on the ages of my kids, but all were involved and knew the upcoming priorities. After they graduated high school and went to college, the meetings became more important. They were sometimes virtual but were normally held during summer and winter holidays when we were all together. At times, there was even an agenda which was collectively made in the months prior to the meeting. Topics included key events happening in everyone's lives, upcoming travel and who needs to be where, and future family priorities. Everyone had a part in it and had input, so all felt involved and committed to make it work.

So, let's get started. We begin with the basics: Budgets, Cashflow, and Net Worth.

Chapter 2 FINANCIAL PLANNING

The goal for a family is not necessarily to earn more, but to net (take home) more. To do this, one has to understand what is coming in and going out and how to maximize value to your benefit. These include knowing all the individual elements of your income and expenses.

2.01 What Is In a Budget?

The first action a family should do is make a budget. Most of us are already good at doing this. Some do it weekly, some monthly, some do it annually – it doesn't matter. It is important to do it to know that you can meet your required expenses.

Once you have a budget, you can then see if your spending stays within the budget you made. If it does, great. If it doesn't, then something needs to change – either your spending or your budget. While it may be easy to change the budget, keep in mind that this may not allow you to reach your goals.

What should be in the budget? Well, that is totally up to you. What are the key expenses that you want to categorize and track on a detailed basis? These can be as simple or as complicated as you want. There are many software programs and phone apps to do this. My preference is just using a normal spreadsheet. The next page illustrates an example of a simple annual budget. Note that some costs are budgeted yearly and some are budgeted monthly.

Monthly Costs	
Item	**US$**
Utility	200
Grocery	750
House items	225
Car Pymt	325
Phone	150
Medical	200
Eating Out	500
Gym	250
House Pymt	1400
Costs/month	4000

Annual Costs	
Item	**US$**
Vacation	4000
Car Ins	700
Other	1000
Sub-total	5700

Costs/year	48000

TOTAL/yr	53700

2.02 Avoid Debt Traps

To further help you make or expand a budget, beware there are many debt traps to entice you to spend more than you can. The most common is credit cards. I am not saying credit cards are bad. But, if you cannot manage your funds to pay off the credit card, then don't use one. The list of debt traps is large, so best you identify the ones that attract you and avoid them.

Here are some helpful tips to help you with your budget.
- Be disciplined – break down your spending into as many different categories as you need.
- Try to save before you spend – decide a fixed amount you want to save each month.

- Automate your savings – once the amount is decided, find a way to automate it from your earnings to avoid the temptation of spending it.
- Take control of your credit card – always pay in full, don't live on 'monthly credit'. It can easily grow out of control. If you cannot handle credit responsibly, pay with cash. For more details on the various credit card fees, read chapter 2.06.
- Track expenses to know where your money is going – this can be done by keeping receipts, logging expenses on your phone, or some banks can also do this for you as part of the electronic statement.

2.03 Elements of Cashflow

In the end, every company hopes to be successful for many years, much like a family. The way to do this is first make a budget (as mentioned above) and then plan your future cashflow.

There are many of us who budget our company's project in detail and plan the project cashflow for years. In some industries, this planning can be for 10-20 years due to the size and duration of the project. Yet, when I ask these same people if they have made a 5-year cashflow for their family, they say no. If you don't, how will you know that you have enough money for a future expense that you may need?

For example: we encourage our kids to do well in school so they can get into a good college. Now, college tuition goes up annually and let's assume your child will graduate in 10 years. They listen, do well, and are smart enough to get admission to a prestigious and expensive university. At this point, you hope you are in a position that you don't have to say "Sorry, you did your part but we can't afford to send you there because we didn't plan for the expense."

Believe me when I say this is not easy and cannot be done at the last minute. All three of my kids attended international primary and secondary schools and private universities in the U.S. for both their undergraduate and graduate degrees. This large annual cash expenditure spread over time needs to be planned so funds are available when needed.

After you have made your budget, the next step is to make your annual cashflow statement. My suggestion for a duration would be a 10-year cashflow, but a 5-year one will also work. It should be done together with your spouse or significant other (if you have one) to ensure everyone is working towards the same goal.

The pushback I normally get on this is 'How do we know what will happen in 5 or 10 years? Things will change.' I agree that we do not know the future – but this does not mean we should not plan. Whether you want to save for a house, buy a new car every four years, pay college tuition fees, etc., you should be able to do it when required. Unless you have made your cashflow, you will not know if there is a shortfall and in what years.

So, what elements should be in a cashflow? These are usually generic and summed at a higher level (not as detailed as a budget). Hence, it is important to categorize the major elements that you want to manage over years. See next page for a cashflow example:

All numbers in thousands

	Yr 1	Yr 2	Yr 3	Yr 4	Yr 5	Yr 6	Yr 7	Yr 8	Yr 9	TOTAL
Housing Costs/yr (1)(2)	48.0	49.4	50.9	52.5	54.0	55.6	57.3	59.0	60.8	487.6
Vacation (2)	4.0	4.1	4.2	4.4	4.5	4.6	4.8	4.9	5.1	40.6
Car Insurance (2)	0.7	0.7	0.7	0.8	0.8	0.8	0.8	0.9	0.9	7.1
Other	1.0	1.0	1.0	1.0	1.0	1.0	1.0	1.0	1.0	9.0
New car				40.0					50.0	90.0
Kids summer camp	4.0		5.0		6.0		7.0		8.0	30.0
College Tuition						15.0	16.0	17.0	18.0	66.0
Tax (Estimated)	15.0	15.0	16.0	16.0	17.0	17.0	18.0	18.0	19.0	151.0
TOTAL Expenses	72.7	70.3	77.9	114.6	83.3	94.1	104.9	100.8	162.8	**881.4**
Salary (3)	85.0	86.7	88.4	90.2	92.0	93.8	95.7	97.6	99.6	829.1
Investments	10.0	10.0	10.0	10.0	10.0	10.0	10.0	10.0	10.0	90.0
Other income	5.0	5.0	5.0	5.0	5.0	5.0	5.0	5.0	5.0	45.0
TOTAL Income	100.0	101.7	103.4	105.2	107.0	108.8	110.7	112.6	114.6	**964.1**
Spare Income	27.3	31.4	25.5	-9.4	23.7	14.8	5.8	11.8	-48.2	**82.8**

(1) This was taken from monthly budget cost ($4000) multiplied by 12
(2) Costs are escalated at 3% to account for inflation
(3) Salary is escalated at 2% to account for (hopefully) getting an annual raise

Your cashflow is a living document and should be updated and revised routinely.

Once you believe your kids are old enough to understand, you should share the cashflow (or portions of it) with them so they are aware of what is happening. When our kids were in high school, we would share the top part (expenses) with them. This involvement also gets them to understand that not everything is easily affordable. The bottom part (income) was shared later after they understood salary and earnings.

Now, how often should you update the cashflow statement? Essentially, as often as you want – but don't make it a tedious effort or you will not want to maintain it. My suggestion is twice a year, or whenever you have a significant change of inflows or outflows happen.

Recently (the last couple of decades), there have been bank funds, insurance options, financial packages that try to 'guarantee future college tuition' or provide you other security by having you deposit a certain amount per year. I agree this is better than nothing. But you are basically outsourcing your cashflow management to a third-party company and giving them a profit to do it. Why not take the time, do it yourself, and keep the profit yourself? You will feel better after doing it and be more comfortable with your personal financial situation.

2.04   How to Calculate Net Worth

All of us have a net worth (assets minus liabilities). It may not be big and it may, unfortunately, be negative for some. But it is important to know your net worth and monitor how it changes over time.

What happens if a company's net worth decreases year-on-year even though they earn money every year? They will eventually liquidate themselves. Likewise, if a family's net worth decreases every year, the family may be left with nothing. Unfortunately, this family who worked hard and earned all their life will retire broke.

Retirement account balances are not increasing fast enough to cover rising life expectancy. Worker's savings, company retirements, and government pensions were not designed for the extra life span that people enjoy. As such, many are drying up faster than expected or the retirement age is being extended. Then, to make matters more difficult, governments and employers have pushed the risk and responsibility for retirement onto individuals by shifting from traditional 'defined benefit pensions' (company takes the risk) to 'defined contribution plans' (employee takes the risk).

These indications further support that families need to take control and plan their financial future themselves for security. It will become increasingly difficult to depend on companies and governments to 'take care of us' in the future.

So, what is net worth and how is it calculated? Net worth is simply an accurate snapshot of your financial situation and is a single number that shows the value of everything you own minus the debts you owe. Basically, it is the value of all your assets minus the value of all your liabilities. Most companies refer to this as 'retained earnings' which you can find on their balance sheet. For us individuals, I will stay with net worth.

Let's list how to do a quick net worth for a typical family:

Assets

Cash in bank		5,000
Bank 1	*2000*	
Bank 2	*3000*	
Funds/Stocks		25,000
Funds	*10000*	
Stocks	*15000*	
House Value		250,000
Jewelry		20,000
Household Items		30,000
Automobiles		40,000
Car 1	*25000*	
Car 2	*15000*	
Total Assets =		**370,000**

Liabilities

House Mortgage	185,000
Credit Card Debt	6,500
Car 1 loan	20,000
Car 2 loan	10,000
Total Liabilities	**221,500**

Net Worth

Total Assets	370,000
Total Liabilities	221,500
NET WORTH :	**148,500**

Financial Planning

Here are some comments regarding net worth:
- For assets, you should use the market value at the present time – not what you paid for it. Certain assets may increase in value (such as a house, deposit accounts, stocks) while certain assets may decrease in value (automobiles, furniture). The value of items will change as you update your sheet.

- For jewelry & precious metals, it may be difficult to get market value. As an estimate, you can sometimes base the value on weight (i.e. for gold) or perhaps use the insured value. As a last resort, you can use half of what you paid. It is up to you to be reasonable.

- For liabilities, list the actual value that you owe.

- When you subtract the two, you get the net worth.

Net worth is always quoted as of a certain date, for example Dec 31, 20XX, because the exact value of your asset and/or liability could technically be different the next day. So, it does not matter what date you pick or how often you choose to update – just do it routinely and periodically. Most people choose December 31 (end of year) and do it annually as that also coincides with the tax reporting year. This is what most companies also report.

What is important is that your net worth should grow over time. Sure, there may be a year where it is down due to a market downturn or a high expense year, but the general trend should be that it is increasing. If it doesn't, you can work your whole life but have little or no value to show for it at the end.

2.05 Is Insurance Important?

Another key element of cash is insurance. We have become a society that insures everything. There is nothing wrong with it, assuming you know what you insure and that the probability of needing the insurance is worth the premium or the peace of mind. What are the different types of insurance that are common for individuals:

- Health Insurance: This is designed to cover medical expenses. If employed full time, the majority cost of this is normally covered by your employer. If it is not, you will need to subsidize the coverage on your own.

- Life Insurance: This insurance provides a payment to designated beneficiaries in the event of your death, to prevent them from suffering hardship after you are gone.

- Auto Insurance: This insurance is to protect your vehicle and damage caused in an accident. There are different parts to the coverage which are explained here and summarized in the table below.
    - Bodily Injury – Pays for the medical costs of the people who are injured (not including yourself) when you are responsible for the accident.
    - Property Damage – Damage that happens to a third party's vehicle and other property, such as fence, building front, public property, etc. Does not cover damage to your own vehicle.
    - Uninsured Motorist – This covers damage (to you or your car) caused by a driver who does not have any or enough insurance (provided they are at fault).

- Medical expense – Covers medical injury to you and those in your car regardless of who is at fault for the accident. As this is similar to Bodily Injury, this coverage is not available everywhere.

- Comprehensive – Helps pay to replace or repair your vehicle if it's stolen or damaged in an incident that's not a collision (such as fire, vandalism, hail, falling tree, etc.).

- Collison – Covers damage caused to your own car.

TYPE OF AUTO INSURANCE AND THEIR COVERAGE						
Type of Auto Insurance	Coverage Applying To:					
	Those in Your Car			Property or Car You Hit		
	Car/Property	Driver	Others	Car/Property	Driver	Others
Bodily Injury Liability		X	X		X	X
Property Damage Liability				X		
Uninsured/underinsured motorist		X	X			
Medical Expense		X	X			
Comprehensive Damage (anything but collision)	X					
Collision Damage	X					

A 'comprehensive' policy (also known as 'full coverage') normally covers all items. If you do not want full coverage, you can usually exclude certain parts from insurance if you don't find value in it. For example, you may not want collision damage on an old car where the premium cost is not worth the expected value. Most countries require third party coverage (damage to others) if you own a car.

- Renter's (or tenant's) Insurance: If you don't own your home, this insurance protects the tenant's belongings in case of theft or damage.

- Homeowner's Insurance: This protects the value of your home and the owner's contents should they get damaged, especially the building's structure. Normally, this is a bank requirement if you own your home with a mortgage and will fire insurance.

It is important to note that all insurances will have some type of financial ceiling (as coverage is unlimited) and require a deductible (you pay a small initial amount, insurance covers the balance). For any insurance you take, you should make sure you understand exactly what is covered, under what circumstances, and to what extent.

Always remember – what is the basic purpose of insurance? It is to cover a large cost at a time when you cannot afford the loss. But, for this protection, you need to pay a premium. If you can *comfortably* cover the loss if/when it occurs, then you do not need insurance. Keep in mind that some places require by law or policy that you must have insurance (i.e. mortgage, car insurance).

But here is an interesting question: if you were not required to have fire insurance on your house, would you still take it? If you did a probability calculation, then it does not make financial sense to take fire insurance as an individual.

Let's assume a $250,000 house in the USA. The premium for fire insurance is on average about $0.35 per year per $1,000 and the probability that your house will burn to the ground is about 1 in 3000 (obviously depends on the area).

Cost of premium = 250,000 ÷ 1000 x $0.35 = $87.5 / year
Amount you will recover from insurance if you house burns
  = $250,000.

Probability you will need the insurance in 20 years
  is 1 ÷ 3000 = 0.033%
Probability payout amount
  = $250,000 x 0.033% = $83 (once in 30 years)

As you can see from the above calculation, it does not make sense to take fire insurance. Statistically, fire insurance is not a good investment for an individual.

Keep in mind the above are ballpark estimates. Insurance costs vary greatly between states or countries based on local costs and varying likelihood of damages. The numbers are not important, it is the principle.

In practice, most people have insurance because they cannot afford another house instantly if their current one burned down. Also, the intrinsic value of the house is more than just the market value – it is the family home and the inconvenience to the family is much more. So, the true value of the house would be much higher (perhaps a factor of 4-6 times) to the family.

This concept (actual value is different than inherent personal value) is called 'utility theory'. It deals with subjective values impacting personal decisions. Risk averse people will make choices in favor of lower risk options, even if they have a lower monetary value. To a family, the 'utility' value of the house is higher than the market value.

Obviously, insurance companies know this as they also do the same calculation. To them, the house value is the market price as they look at it without emotion and no utility. So, you having insurance is financially a good deal for them.

Insurance exists for an eventuality you are not currently able to cover. It should be taken for the right reasons and with the understanding of its true value to you (even if emotional). Only then is it worth paying the premium. However, if your cashflow is planned carefully, you may be able to avoid insurance premiums.

2.06   Credit cards and fees

Credit cards are continuously a debated topic – are they good or bad? They are the most common method of payment and can easily be linked to your mobile wallet. It is well known that consumers who pay with credit cards spend more than if they were paying with cash, which is why businesses that accept credit cards have increased sales.

Credit cards allow you to purchase items 'on credit', which can be beneficial if part of your cashflow plan. Buying on credit is paying for something later than when you actually bought it. The problems with credit cards are impulse buying and not knowing how you will pay for your purchases when payment is due.

I believe credit cards are good, assuming you pay off the card when it is due. They allow you to make purchases and benefit from their use while you hold the cash temporarily until the payment is due. Some offer warranty extensions, rewards, points, travel perks, etc. And, if managed properly, they help build a good credit score, which can benefit future loans or rental applications.

But many people get mired in credit card debt because they're not mindful about how to use it, forget about charges they made a month ago, or what fees are involved. Credit card fees might be unpleasant, but they're still important to understand, especially if you're dealing with credit card debt. Let's look at some of the most common fees:

- Annual fee – An annual fee is charged once a year for the convenience of having a credit card. Some credit card companies waive the annual fee during the first year. Some cards' annuals fees are worth it because they provide other tangible benefits (airline miles, travel credit, discounts, etc.) or perks (lounge access, priority services, etc.) to offset the fee.

- Finance charge – This is a monthly interest charge (around 18% per year which equals 1.5% per month) charged to your account on the outstanding balance beyond your credit card's grace period. To get this high interest, banks are happy when you pay in installments or only the minimum amount due. For example, if your card outstanding balance is $1000 and you don't pay it, the bank will charge you 1.5% x $1000 = $15 per month which adds up to $180 per year.

- Late fee – This is a charge when you fail to make your minimum payment by the due date. Late fees are charged once for every billing cycle you are late.

- Cash Advance fee – This is charged when you use your credit card to get cash and is normally a percentage of the transaction. Credit cards should be used to make payments. Debit cards should be used for cash withdrawals.

Remember, credit card companies make money off fees. The convenience of having and using a credit card comes with costs if you are not careful. Fees are bank specific and are sometimes negotiable depending on your activity, bank balances, and relationship with the bank.

In addition, refunds on credit cards are not immediate. While a credit card purchase may only take seconds, the reversal or refund may take anywhere from 2 to 30 days. Refunds require several steps and depend on many factors.

However, as you are not billed for credit card activity until (usually) one month later, it is easier to dispute charges on a credit card before funds leave your account. In contrast, debit cards funds are withdrawn from your account immediately upon use.

Credit cards are extremely useful, so long as you don't abuse them. The key is to be smart about your finances so you can make the most out of your credit cards and avoid paying unnecessary fees.

Credit card companies do a lot of marketing to entice you to their card and there are a lot of options available. When choosing a card, weigh the different fees against the possible benefits and perks as explained above.

However, keep the number of credit cards you have to a minimum. This will make it easier to manage and consolidate since, for each card, you should validate every charge on the statement to make sure it is correct. This will help you track your expenses and hopefully avoid any possible fraud.

2.07 Planning for emergencies

Saving for an emergency supports financial wellness and can be just as important as investing for long-term goals. A common rule of thumb suggests that households should have three to six months' worth of expenses set aside for unexpected expenses. Emergency savings can be a combination of cash and liquidity (ability to convert an asset into cash quickly).

Not all emergencies are alike and are broken into 2 categories of financial shocks: spending shocks and income shocks.

- Spending shocks – These encompass a wide range of expenses that share two defining characteristics: they are unplanned and unwanted. A spending shock could be anything from uncovered health care costs, major home repairs, or other unplanned expenses.
- Income shocks – Usually, these are unexpected job loss or other reduction in income. This is less likely to occur than a spending shock for most households, but can have more severe financial consequences.

While all shocks are unpredictable, spending shocks are more likely to occur as a matter of course while income shocks are generally expected to be less frequent. Setting aside an appropriate amount of funds can help mitigate the potential harm of unanticipated expenses, helping you avoid expensive emergency financing and offering peace of mind.

The goal of a well-planned emergency fund is to turn potential crises into manageable setbacks. Planning for both types of shocks is important and requires different strategies. However, holding too much in cash can be a drag on a portfolio's ability to meet long-term financial goals.

Choosing whether to save for retirement or build up a contingency fund can be challenging. Appropriately managing the risks of unforeseen circumstances can provide the freedom to invest with a higher risk-return trade-off to build wealth for longer-term goals.

2.08 Having Financial Goals

Now, why bother doing everything that is mentioned above? Quite simply – so you are able to reach your financial goals. But what financial goals? If you are not able to answer this question, then it is all the more critical for you to learn and follow the aforementioned.

As with any entity, whether it is a company or a family, there are financial needs that are required for the future. We all want to be able to enjoy a certain lifestyle throughout our life, and achieving that requires money at each stage.

Here is a typical conversation that happens when I pose this question to people:
  Me: Do you have financial goals?
  Other: Yes, I want to be rich!
        (while this sounds good, it does not mean anything)
  Me: What do you mean you want to be rich?
  Other: I want a lot of money
  Me: How much is a lot?
  Other: A million dollars
  Me: Okay, by when?
  Other: As soon as possible

As you can see this is not a realistic discussion. Yes, theoretically it is possible (win the lottery, develop a new invention, win Wimbledon, etc.). But the odds of achieving it are so remote that few would risk all they have to achieve it.

So, financial goals for most of us need to be realistic and should have a high probability of being achieved. Here are examples of some financial goals:

Financial Planning

- I would like to have a net worth of $X dollars at age 65 so I can retire with peace of mind.
- I would like to have a sustainable cashflow without having to depend on my current job.
- I need to have $X available in 10 years so that I can send my child to a private university.

When I was young, my personal financial goal was growth to reach a point to maintain the same standard of living without having to depend on a paycheck. Later, when the kids were in high school, the goal became to have cash to finance their college when needed. Finally, when most family financial obligations were filled, the goal became value preservation, mainly for retirement. At this point, it was more important to take less risk so that cash remains available for our future.

All financial goals should be specific so they can be measured and should be planned so they can be achieved. If you are not able to sort this yourself, my advice is to hire a financial planner in your area that can help you.

Now that you have your finances in order and a financial plan to get there, let's talk about some basic investing principles.

Chapter 3 INVESTING

After you have sorted your budget, cashflow, net worth, and made financial goals, you are ready to start investing. You may think you don't have money to invest. Well, just as we make time (not have time) for the important things in our life, you should also make money available for investing (as you will never have spare money). This may mean giving up on a current financial desire to help get the future you want. Hence, this should be part of your cashflow.

This chapter is not about 'where' to invest but more about 'how' to invest. There are many other books and materials about where to invest – the most common investments are real estate and stocks. There are others such as commodities, foreign exchange, trust deeds, cryptocurrency, starting a business, etc. While all may sound promising, make sure you fully understand the investment you are making before you put your hard-earned money into it. There is no guarantee in any investment. I personally chose real estate and mutual funds as my main investments.

Just like a company uses many different criteria to decide where to invest, families should also decide what criteria to use for themselves. Is the goal cashflow, capital growth, better return, short payout, etc.? Each of these is valid and accomplishes a different goal. While I explain some of these basic terms below, I advise further research to understand the terminology before moving forward with your investment.

3.01   Investment Goals

- Cashflow goal – This type of investment would return annual cashback on your investment. Examples of this are interest accounts, property rental, dividend stocks, and fixed deposit accounts.

- Capital growth goal – This investment says you invest up front and you will get your money back in a large lump sum sometime in the future. Examples of this are stocks, antiques, commodities, and land.

- Savings goal – Wanting a certain bank balance at a specified point in time.

- Emergency Fund – Money to cover an unplanned emergency as explained in section 2.07.

Obviously, there are investments that are a combination of the above.

3.02 What are Investment Criteria

- Payout – This is defined as a time element (normally years) and is the amount of time it will take for you to breakeven on your investment. In other words, at what point do your positive cashflows make up for negative cash investment? For example, if you invest $100 and will make $12/year, your breakeven is 8.3 years. Any money made after that is your profit.

- Rate of Return (ROR) – This is the gain (or loss) compared to the cost of one initial investment. You buy/invest in an asset today and then sell that asset in the future – for example buying and selling a house. The return you made on the asset is your ROR, typically expressed in the form of a percentage. When the ROR is positive, it is considered a gain and when the ROR is negative, it reflects a loss on the investment.

- Internal Rate of Return (IRR) – While ROR is the gain (or loss) compared to the cost of one initial investment and one future sale, IRR is similar and compares investments with various annual cashflows that have different time horizons. – for example buying a house, renting it for a few years, and then selling it.

- Profit/Investment Ratio – Profit investment ratio (PIR), also known as profitability index (PI), is the ratio of payoff to the proposed investment. It is a useful tool for ranking investments because it allows you to quantify the amount of value created per unit of investment and compare projects. You should aim for a PIR above 1.

The few terms above are generic and apply to all investments. Some are used interchangeably (for example IRR and ROR). You can easily search the internet to find out more about these terms and others that are used. Each term measures a different aspect of investments. Depending on your situation, you should use the term that will meet the goals you want.

Businesses and companies are notorious for inventing terms and ratios that make them look good. So, make it a point to understand what is in the underlying calculation they use to determine the ratio. But one thing companies are good at is being very clear on what investment criteria they use. In other words, when they need to make an investment, they know and identify the key term or ratio they will measure to determine whether or not a project should be pursued. One may use PIR while another may use IRR. Both can give different results depending on the magnitude of the investment. *What criteria do you currently use for your own investments?* This question also stumps some when I ask them. As individuals, we should also be clear about what criteria we use (like a business).

Which one you use is up to you, but you should know why you are using that one. My personal criteria is IRR, as this made it simple for me to compare different investments.

There is one last item I will mention here but not dwell upon: remember to think about tax incentives when investing. Different governments around the world treat investments differently. Some may give you a benefit for certain category investments, how to handle depreciation, tax on capital gains, etc. Just make sure what you do is legal and will stand up to the local laws as they vary. For more details on this, some research or speaking to a tax specialist is recommended.

3.03   Time Value of Money

Imagine you are driving on a long straight road that is aligned with similar nice trees on both sides. As you are driving and admiring the view, did you notice that even though all the trees are the same, they have a different 'beauty' value? The trees that are very near to you are big, majestic, and look the most beautiful. Yet that exact same tree much further down the road is tiny and has very little value to you. Well folks, money is the same.

Money that is near to the current time is worth more than the same money many years from now. In other words, $1 today is worth more than $1 ten years in the future. There are two main reasons for this:
1. Inflation – as the cost of goods goes up, the purchasing power of your money decreases.
2. Opportunity to invest – hopefully, you can do something with the $1 today (i.e. invest) so that it grows to more than that, hence you will have more than $1 ten years from now.

Here is another interesting question I ask: "*If someone gave you one cent ($0.01) on the first day of the month and it doubled every day. How much would you have at the end of the month?*" While we can all take out a calculator or spreadsheet to figure this out (please don't do that), what do you think the answer is? How much do you feel is the amount? A few hundred? I will give you the answer later in this chapter to not spoil the surprise now.

All of this leads to an important concept called 'Time Value of Money' (TVM). The purpose of this section is to show you how to calculate TVM, so you keep it in mind when looking at your cashflow needs and financial goals.

Note this is only a simple introduction and not a detailed explanation or analysis. There are a lot of different ways TVM can be used – in fact there are entire books alone written on this topic. Essentially all business and investments use this philosophy to determine the quality of an investment. So, my purpose is to explain the basic calculation, show a couple examples, and hope you keep it in mind for yourself. For those that want to learn more, I strongly encourage you to pursue it further.

(a) Calculation

The basic equation for TVM is as follows:

$$FV = PV \times (1 + R)^t \quad \text{or} \quad PV = \frac{FV}{(1 + R)^t}$$

Where:
  FV = Future Value amount ($)
  PV = Present Value today ($)
  R = rate of discount (Percentage or decimal) per period
  t = Time period

Investing

(Note that R and t must be in the same units. For example, if t is in years than R must be rate/year)

(b) Define variables R & t

't' is the time period that you want to evaluate. In other words, what is the time span that the money will be inflated or deflated. The units for t can be days or months but is usually years as investment and financial decisions are normally over many years.

'R' is the rate for discount that should be applied during the period. Now what determines R? The most obvious is inflation. To determine what $5000 in the future is worth today, you could use inflation as the discount rate. Alternatively, if you deposited $4000 into an account today that gave you 5% annual return, you can calculate what that account will be worth in the future. What rate you want to use for R is up to you. It depends on what you want to measure and what affects it.

(c) Examples

How much is $25,000 received in 2025 worth in 2021 if inflation is 4%?
   Using above equation: PV = $25,000 ÷ $(1+0.04)^4$ = $21,370

If I have $15,000 today and invest it at 6%/year, how much will it become 7 years from now?
   FV = $15,000 x $(1+0.06)^7$ = $22,554

Assume you have a choice of receiving $25,000 today or $30,000 three years from now. You believe you could invest the $25,000 at 7% return. Which do you take?
   PV = $30,000 ÷ $(1+0.07)^3$ = $24,489 < $25,000 or
   FV = $25,000 x $(1+0.07)^3$ = $30,626 > $30,000

So, you would take the $25,000 today. But if you did not understand TVM, you could have made the wrong decision.

To take this one step further, if you have a project or investment that has different cashflows over different periods of time, you will still use TVM to determine its 'net' PV. To do this properly, you need to understand the different time horizons and use an appropriate discount rate.

3.04   Investing vs. Gambling

It's important to understand the difference between these two terms. You should know how and why you are investing; else you are essentially gambling.

Here is an interesting conversation that I sometimes have during my sessions:

    Me: *How many of you gamble?*
        Hesitantly, a few hands go up.
        I then ask a different question…
    Me: *How many of you invest?*
        Not surprisingly, almost everyone's hand goes up.
        Now I ask the interesting question…
    Me: *What's the difference?*

The answers I usually get are 'Gambling is short term', 'Gambling is small investment for big gain', 'Gambling is putting money at risk without any tangible asset', etc.

Most people don't realize the difference. We all like to believe we are good investors and not gamblers. Gambling has a negative connotation because of its perception. But, if you did not research or understand your investment, then you are basically gambling and hoping for a good outcome. Essentially, every investment is a gamble in some form, so we all gamble. You are putting up some money (or time or effort) with the hope of getting more back in the future.

Now, let's look at the difference. A commonly held view is that a gamble is exclusively a game of chance – you have no ability to control the outcome or the probability of possible return. An investment, on the other hand, is a risk weighted probability-based gamble. There may be options to change something during the investment, modify the timing, or find some other way to enhance the return (i.e. transfer the stock, claim tax benefits) or limit your downside (get out early, swap with something else). In any case, if you do not know what you are doing with an investment or how it works, I believe you are gambling.

The most common forms of gambling are the lottery, raffles, slot machines, etc. The probability of winning is fixed by the owner and cannot be changed by you. Yes, you can buy more tickets or play more times, but the odds of each ticket does not change and the drawing date is normally fixed. Similarly, there are many forms of risking money - stocks, property, commodities, cards, dice, etc. Surprisingly, people have different views whether these are investing or gambling. One that is often debated is playing cards.

Some believe that playing cards is gambling while others, who know how to play, do not. If you understand probability, how to bet, and people's reactions, then you can successfully play cards for a profit. There is a Hollywood movie called *"21"* which shows how a group of college kids devise a system to beat casinos. Likewise, there are "professional" gamblers who make a living by 'gambling'. Hence, they are not gambling because they know what they are doing.

3.05 Buying a House and/or Car

While growing up, most of us are taught that one goal in life is to eventually become a homeowner and/or have a nice car. Yes, it is a great level of personal satisfaction to be able to own one or both of these. So, let's look at these assets.

House: Buying a home is a major financial commitment and no matter how many times you crunch the numbers, it can be difficult to make the leap. There are a number of factors to weigh before taking the decision, but the primary consideration is that your overall financial health should not suffer after the purchase. Many people make this big purchase without fully understanding the true costs. By doing so, they undermine the hard work they have already done to build their financial portfolio and security.

The thinking used to be: Buy a house when you are in your twenties, keep making payments, and then the house would be fully yours when you retire. Hence you have no house payment then. But in today's transient society, this philosophy may not apply. So before you get wrapped up in making this a priority, it is important to understand the financing and housing market and if it is really the best decision for you.

Owning a home comes with many costs that homebuyers may not be aware of such as closing costs, homeowner's insurance costs, maintenance & repair costs, association dues, property taxes, etc. See the tables on the next page.

BUY A HOUSE

PROS	CONS
• Monthly bank payment is fixed for the loan • Interest may be tax deductible • Can build up equity with your payments • Depending on the local market and economy, the asset value of the house may go up (appreciate) • Pride of ownership • Make own improvements	• You will need to make a down payment (+/- 20%) • Normally will need a loan (may require good credit score) which will require interest payments • All repairs, insurance costs, and maintenance are yours - can be high depending on house age • Most properties have some type of additional monthly 'service' fees • May limit mobility if you need to quickly sell before moving • All house risks are yours (fire, structure, etc.) – although insurance available • Depending on the local market and economy, the asset value of the house may go down (depreciate)

RENT A HOUSE

PROS	CONS
• Less cash required up front • Monthly payment is fixed during the lease • All repairs and maintenance are normally landlord responsibility	• Rent may increase with the market • If you get a bad landlord, may be difficult to get repairs done • You do not build equity

Car: Having a car gives a great sense of freedom and pride, especially after you get your driving license. However, for the younger generation (those in their twenties) and the ones living in major cities, the charm of car ownership is reducing.

BUY A CAR

PROS	CONS
• Monthly payment is fixed • Interest may be tax deductible • Freedom to have transportation at your disposal whenever you need	• You will need to make a down payment (+/- 20%) • Normally will need a loan (may require good credit score) which will require interest payments • A car is a depreciating asset. Hence, the value of it will go down (new cars - typically 50% in 3 years) • Parking and insurance costs • All repairs and maintenance are yours - can be high depending on car age

RIDE SHARING / PUBLIC TRANSPORT

PROS	CONS
• No cash outlay up front • No monthly payment • Pay for only what you use • No parking hassles	• May not always be available when you need, harder during peak periods • May be difficult to attend events as you are dependent on others

Investing

In both cases of a house and a car, the emotional satisfaction and pride of ownership still remain, but should not be the only factor. You should make an informed calculation of whether buying is the best option for you from a financial standpoint or not. Carefully consider whether paying the high initial down payment, monthly loan payments, and other costs are a better decision than renting or leasing? If not, you can then see if happiness justifies the extra cost of ownership.

3.06   Types of Bank Accounts

There are many different types of bank accounts as most of us know since we already have 1 or more. As with any financial decision, it is important to understand the difference between them to determine which accounts are beneficial and necessary and which are not.

- Current or Checking account – A current account is mostly used for routine financial transactions. You will be issued a debit card and a check book for making purchases or cash withdrawals. The account can be used to receive salaries and some banks allow you to maintain different currency accounts. The account may have a monthly maintenance fee or have minimum balance requirements you need to meet to avoid the fee.

- Savings account – This is a deposit account that can be used to hold money you don't plan to spend right away. These accounts are not designed for everyday spending or paying bills and usually offer higher interest rates than checking accounts.

- Money Market Account (MMA) – This typically allows earning higher interest on balances. But, to offer higher interest rates, banks set a limit on the number of monthly transactions allowed so make sure you check the rules. In addition, the account may require you to maintain a higher balance to avoid fees.

- Certificate of Deposit (CD) – These are time deposit accounts. It's with the understanding that you'll leave your savings in place for a set time period. This is called the maturity term and, during this time, you'll earn interest on your balance. Once the CD matures, you can either withdraw your initial deposit along with interest earned or roll the entire amount over to a new CD. Withdrawing your money before maturity term can trigger penalties and/or fees.

3.07 Loans and interest

Loans and debt are part of life. Why? Because there are times when we will not have the funds to do what we need or want, especially large purchases. But this does not mean we should be scared of getting a loan.

Getting a loan should be part of a financial plan. In fact, certain debt can even amplify your returns by allowing you to invest in an opportunity you otherwise could not. If you can make a higher return on an investment than the cost of the loan, you should do it assuming you have considered all the other risks.

All loans require a repayment of both the principal and interest. How these are calculated and administered depends on the loan, what asset is used to secure the loan (known as collateral), and who made the loan (bank, private person, car dealership, etc.). Let's discuss some of the most common loan options.

Flat interest
The interest and sum payable on a loan are calculated at the start of the repayment schedule and does not change until the loan has been paid off. This is the easiest interest to understand.

For example, let's take a loan of $12,000 for 12 months at 6% interest/year. This means a monthly payment of $1,000 to pay back the loan (without interest). Now, add the flat rate of interest at 6%, which equals $720 per year ($12000 x 6% = $720/year = $60/month). Hence, the total monthly payment will be $1060 for 12 months to payback the loan with the interest.

Reducing interest
Here the interest payment reduces every time the borrower makes a payment on the loan balance. The reducing rate of interest considers the reduction in the principal amount after each instalment is paid. The interest percentage (which remains the same) is applied to a reduced amount every month. This results in different instalment amounts each month.

Again, let's take a loan of $12,000 for 12 months at 6% interest/yr. Now, 6% per year equals 0.5% per month. This interest is charged on the 'remaining' loan value.

Month	Loan	Loan Repay	Interest Owed	Total
	12000			
1	11000	1000	60	1060
2	10000	1000	55	1055
3	9000	1000	50	1050
4	8000	1000	45	1045
5	7000	1000	40	1040
6	6000	1000	35	1035
7	5000	1000	30	1030
8	4000	1000	25	1025
9	3000	1000	20	1020
10	2000	1000	15	1015
11	1000	1000	10	1010
12	0	1000	5	1005

For the first month, interest is owed on the $12000 remaining balance. This is 0.5% x 12000 = $60. A loan payment of $1000 has also been made. Now, the remaining balance is $11000. The interest on this is 0.5% x 11000 = $55. The table above shows each month.

Fixed payment or amortization
Another approach is essentially a combination of reducing interest with maintaining a fixed payment. This is most common for mortgages and home loans, normally referred to as amortization.

The calculation sets a monthly fixed payment to pay back both the principal and interest. The interest owed will be reduced as the outstanding balance is reduced. So, in the early years, a higher proportion of the payment will be applied to the interest. In the later years, a higher proportion will apply to the principal. The benefit of amortization is the monthly payment always remains fixed which is why it is appealing to homeowners.

Let's go through this with the equation and an example. Here is the equation:

The basic equation for amortization is as follows:

$$P = L \left(\frac{i}{(1+i)^n - 1} + i \right)$$

Where:
- P = Payment due per period ($)
- L = Loan value ($)
- i = interest rate per period
- n = number of periods

    Note that i & n must be in the same units (month, years, etc.)

Here is an example: Let's take a home loan of $100,000 for 15 years at 6% interest/year. For the above equation....

   L = $100,000
   i = 6%/year = 0.5%/month
   n = 15 years = 180 months

When you put the above values into the equation, the result is that P = $843.86 = monthly payment required. Next, if you were to make a monthly payment table for the loan, it would look like this:

Month	Payment	Interest Paid	Loan Repay	Loan Balance
				100000
1	844	500	344	99656
2	844	498	346	99311
3	844	497	347	98963
4	844	495	349	98614
5	844	493	351	98264
↓	844	↓	↓	↓
	844			
176	844	21	823	3334
177	844	17	827	2507
178	844	13	831	1676
179	844	8	835	840
180	844	4	840	0

As you can see, for the same monthly payment, interest is higher in the early years while loan repayment is higher in the later years. There are many software programs that can do the calculation and make the above table instantly.

Debt consolidation

If you have many different loans to pay, burgeoning credit card bills, or other debts, you can consider debt consolidation. This is basically taking a new loan, preferably at a lower interest rate, to pay off all your other loans. This would help manage the debt and help you repay the loan in affordable monthly instalments. At the least, it should save on interest and perhaps avoid the high penalties levied on card payments. Be careful not to take on new debt from the previous paid off sources, as this only leads to a deeper debt hole.

Prepayment penalty

Banks make loans with the understanding that they intend to recover a certain amount of interest. So, if you want to pay back your loan earlier (to remove the debt), the bank will lose out on the interest. To offset this, some banks add a prepayment penalty into the loan contract. This penalty is an extra amount owed in case you prepay the loan. If this clause exists, make sure you do the cost-benefit analysis of paying your loan off early.

When to not pay off debt
There are 2 main reasons to not pay debt.
- If you are cash poor and need the money to sustain your or your family's well-being, it may be better to keep paying the installments and not pay lump sum cash. Having money for financial hardships or your emergency fund may be wiser than paying off a loan and could prevent you from taking another loan.
- If you have an investment opportunity that gives you higher returns than the interest you are paying, do not pay off the loan. For example, if your loan interest is 4% but your investment is making you 7%, you are better keeping the money in the investment.

While there may be other reasons, they are usually minor compared to the above 2 reasons.

3.08   Summary Points

Now, what is the answer to the 1 cent doubling every day question asked earlier in section 3.03? You will be surprised to know that the answer is $5 after 10 days, $5000 after 20 days, $5.37 million dollars for a 30-day month, and $10.74 million dollars for a 31-day month. I am sure most of you felt the answer was only a few thousand or tens of thousand dollars for the whole month. Now, no one will give you this kind of return. But I pose this question to get you thinking about the power of money growing if you start investing early. You want to be at a point where money works for you instead of you working for money.

I am fortunate that my father sat me down to invest early. After graduating college and in my first job, I was excited to get my first paycheck. I remember my dad asking:
Dad: "So Arvind, what are you going to do with your first paycheck?"
Me (after toiling through college) responded: "Spend it and enjoy!"
Dad: "No you're not. Enjoy some of it but let's discuss how to invest some of it now."

I thought it was harsh at the time, but I'm glad he did. After investing early and for many years, the money has grown to make my future better and provided financial security for my family.

The earlier you understand investments and your needs, the more financially secure you will be in the long run. Having a job or source of income is necessary to provide for yourself and your family. But a job will rarely make you financially secure for your own future, it will essentially 'pay the bills.'

The reason is we generally start living a lifestyle that fits the salary we get (the more we earn, the more we spend, the better we live). What we forget is that we should invest early in life to allow us a more luxurious future instead of splurging now at the expense of future comfort. It is important to budget money for investment, invest on your own, and invest early so it grows.

One should not be scared to invest. While having money in savings is nice and can provide quick emergency funds if needed, bank accounts will not give the return you need to keep up with inflation.

Investing

Finally, some simple points of advice:
- Be clear on your investment goals from the start.

- Don't overextend yourself – invest within reason and do not risk your own well-being in the name of greed. Know the amount of risk you can tolerate. Start small but start!

- Start as early as you can – the compounding effect will benefit you in the future.

- Learn all you can about the investment – don't just dive into it unknowingly. That's essentially gambling.

- Be realistic in your expected return and timing – do not expect to get rich overnight. Understand the risk/reward relationship. Remember – if it sounds too good to be true, it most likely is. Don't let your emotions confuse the realistic outcomes.

- Remember to take into account the tax implications, if any, and consider investment levers which could perhaps lower the tax.

- Make investment decisions based on fact, not emotion.

- Keep your portfolio diversified – remember the old common saying "don't put all your eggs in one basket." No matter how good the return, do not invest all your money in one place. Should that one investment go bust, you will lose everything. Invest in different types of investments – short term, long term, asset based, fund based, etc.

You do not have to be an intellectual genius. Everyone can and should invest to allow their money to grow. Most important – if you still are not sure and want to get involved in a new market, get help from an investment expert.

Chapter 4 DECISION MAKING

After a company has set their cashflow, budgeting goals, and understood how and where to invest their earned money, the next step is having a process to make decisions in the company, especially when key shareholders disagree. Likewise, the family should also have a system for making decisions. This chapter is to present the important concept EMV (Expected Monetary Value) by using decision trees for decision making. It is an excellent tool to make decisions logically, not emotionally.

4.01   What is Decision Analysis

In all situations, there is an element of making a decision. These decisions can be simple (what to have for dinner, should I watch TV, etc.), somewhat more complicated (where to go for vacation, which school to enroll the kids, etc.), or a decision that requires some type of analysis (should we buy a house, should I change jobs, should I invest in my relative's business, etc.). In all of these, you need to have some process or methodology to make the decision. Have you considered all the positives and negatives of each option and the probability of what could happen?

Most decisions we take as individuals are based on 'either-or' outcomes or 'if-then-else' outcomes:
- Either-or-outcomes: This is the normal two prong decision of either I can do option A or I can do option B. We will normally choose the one which gives us the most value. That value can be happiness (dinner), least risk (taking a vacation), or a higher monetary value (changing jobs).
- If-then-else outcomes: These apply when there needs to be a trigger to cause us to take the decision. IF something happens, THEN we can do option A, ELSE we do option B. For example,

IF it is sunny tomorrow, THEN we go for a picnic, ELSE we will go bowling.

Normally, the decisions we make are all or nothing. In other words, we cannot partially make a decision. For example, we cannot partially go on a picnic or eat half a dinner at one place and half at another. Also, the decisions we routinely make are normally fully in our control – hence there is no probability that can be assigned to sway our decision. We believe that we make decisions based on logic or rationale, but we normally make them on emotion.

But what if the decisions became complicated and had many 'if-then-else' scenarios that affected each other? What if there were a calculated probability that would influence the decision? How would you account for this? The rest of this chapter addresses these questions through what are called Decision Trees. It is important to understand Decision Trees for investing purposes, but the concept can be used for any decision.

4.02   Decision Tree Basics

So, what exactly is a decision tree? It is basically a diagram to help visualize the various decision routes that can be taken. Once you have all the decisions and outcomes on paper, it is normally easier to view all the options. These are used in business all the time, so why not at home? The quality of decisions is just as important for the family. For simple decisions, we instinctively do the tree in our head.

Let's now discuss the basics of a decision tree. First, what does the tree look like? Here is an example of a generic decision tree.

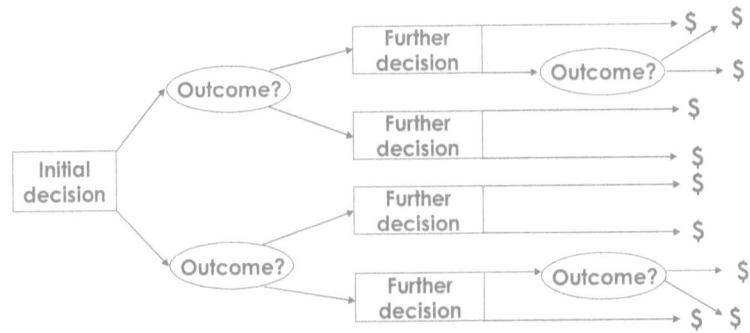

The key elements to remember when drawing the tree:

- Decisions (squares) and chances (ellipses or circles) must be drawn in chronological sequence starting with a decision today. The squares are those decisions that **are** in your control – you can choose what to do. The circles are outcomes that **are not** in your control and are dependent on some external factor. Normally, circles will have a probability associated with it.

- The technique is powerful when later decisions depend on the outcome of earlier ones.

- Paths from chance circles must cover all relevant outcomes and their probability options **must** total 100%. Label clearly all paths and branches to avoid confusion.

- Once you have drawn the full tree left-to-right, the next step is to assign a number to the right. The number at the end of the path represents the total value of the relevant path.

- Roll back the tree right-to-left as follows: At decision squares, retain the branch number with the highest value; at chance circles, take the probabilistically weighted average of the branch values, which is the EMV (described in next section).

Decision Making

- Once you start down one path of the tree (decided that is the way you want to go), the other paths are no longer an option.

We subconsciously take decisions all the time using decision trees, but may not realize it.

Example 1: Dinner Decision

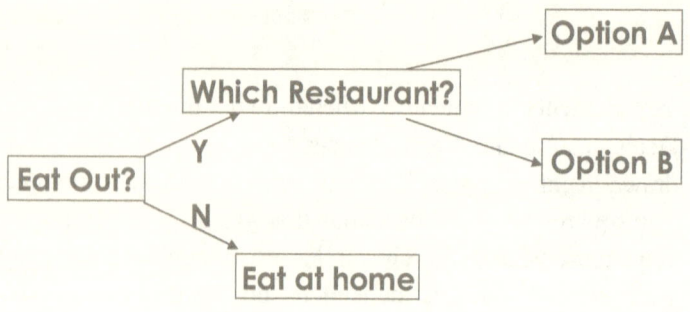

Example 2: Weekend Plans

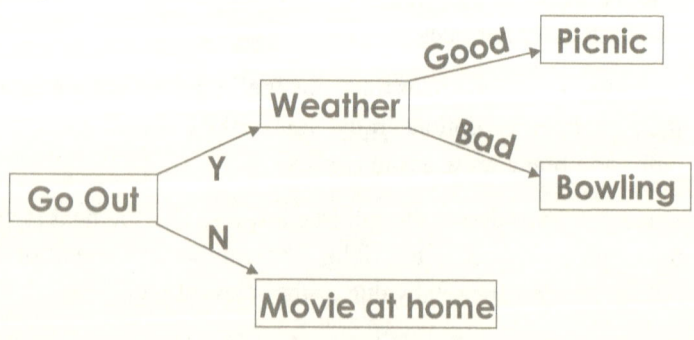

I used decision trees often with the family, especially at our board meetings (as explained in section 1.02). We used them to talk through important decisions that affected all of us (such as house moves, college decisions, my early retirement, etc.). It can be an added agenda item for family board meetings which adds a lot of value.

4.03   Expected Monetary Value

To further expand on the concept, we now introduce a concept called Expected Monetary Value (EMV). Why do we need this? Because not every decision is in our control and may have a probability associated with it. It is a method for combining the basic economic value analysis with a quantitative assessment of uncertainty to yield a risk-adjusted decision. The likelihood of this probability may affect the decision we eventually take.

The calculation of EMV is straightforward and is the mathematical sum of all the options available.

Example 3: Flipping a Coin
   Someone offers you the option of flipping a coin. If it is heads, you win $2. If it is tails, you lose $1. Should you take the flip? What is the EMV?

The EMV of taking the flip is +$0.50 (50% of +$2.00 plus 50% of -$1.00 = +$0.50). The value of not taking the flip is $0. So, yes you should take the flip.

The magnitude of the numbers is also a factor. We would all probably do it if it was the $1 and $2. But, if all the numbers were multiplied by 1000 or 1 million, you may choose not to take the flip because you cannot afford the large loss, regardless of the upside gain. The probability or calculation does not change. So, even though it may be a good decision to take based on the numbers, your own affordability or limited risk profile may prohibit it.

Example 4: Spare Money

You have $10,000 and want to decide what to do with it. The options you have are:
1. Put it in the bank, earn 4% on your money after 1 year.
2. Buy 1000 shares of ABC stock at $10/share. You have read (or researched) there is a 40% chance the stock will go up to $15/share and a 60% chance the stock will go down to $8/share (both after 1 year).
3. Buy 40 raffle tickets at $250/ticket. Each ticket has a 1 in a 2000 chance of winning a $100,000 house. The raffle will be held after 1 year.

What is your best profit option based on EMV?

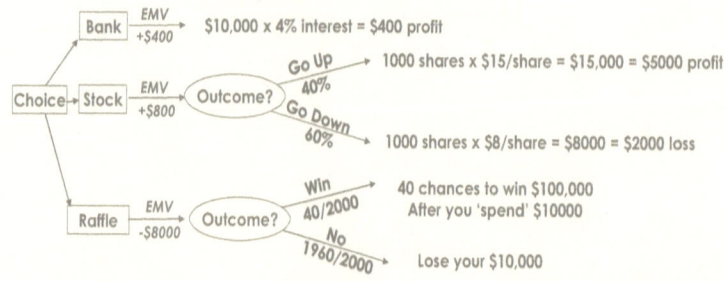

Family as a Business

EMV calculations:
1. Bank: As there is no probability here, the EMV is the profit of $400
2. Stock: EMV = [40% x $5000 = $2000] plus [60% x -$2000 = -$1200] = +$800
3. Lottery: EMV = [(40 ÷ 2000) x ($100,000-$10,000)] plus [(1960 ÷ 2000) x -$10,000] = -$8000

Based on the above, the best option would be the stock.

The EMV calculation is sensitive to the values you have for the profit and loss along with the probability of occurrence. So, it is important to do proper research to be comfortable with the risks. For example, the bank may be lower risk, but is also lower return. However, this does not mean you should not invest in stocks. The future is always unknown and the alternative is to just hold on to your money and do nothing with it. While this may seem to be a safe risk averse solution, your financial future will also not grow.

Example 5: Lottery Example

We have all dreamed about winning the big prize lottery. However, using EMV and working through the math shows that a lottery ticket is not a good purchase.

Let's take a lottery system that has 55 numbered balls where 6 are drawn at random. If you match all 6 numbers, you win $5 million jackpot, 5 numbers win $50000, and so on (see table). The cost of the lottery ticket is $2.

Take each prize, multiply the net return by the probability of winning, add all those values to get the probabilistic amount, and then subtract the price of the ticket to get the expected value.

# matching	Probability	Prize Money	Prob x Prize
0	0.4823722929	0	0.00
1	0.3946682396	0	0.00
2	0.1096300666	2	0.22
3	0.0127107324	25	0.32
4	0.0006084925	500	0.30
5	0.0000101415	50000	0.51
6	0.0000000345	5000000	0.17

Probabilistic winning amount	1.52
Cost of buying lottery ticket	2.00
Expected value of purchase	**-0.48**

We end up with a negative EMV of -$0.48, which suggests it does not make sense to buy a ticket. Furthermore, this does not take into account multiple winners (prize gets shared), or tax owed on the winnings. These will then further reduce the expected value.

Since you have no control on the odds of winning, the lottery is gambling, not investing. And, if buying a lottery ticket is a predicted net loss to the buyer, it is a net gain to the seller (normally the government). This is why governments like lottery systems and design them to be in their favor. In principle, they are getting a voluntary tax.

It is exciting to hear when people win the lottery. We all think 'Why can't that be me?" But for every winner, there were tens of thousands of losers. Keep that in mind next time you want to buy a ticket.

Summary
As explained above, decision trees can become as simple or as complicated as you want to make them. The squares and circles can

keep going as far as needed – which is okay. These trees are very powerful and I suggest you use them. Why? All the decisions, probabilities, and outcomes are written down and can be visualized with the various paths that can happen. Getting the tree made and agreed by all is a large step in getting to a better decision in which everyone can agree.

The purpose of the above was to introduce the important concept of how to make a decision tree. An added discussion to the EMV tree could be 'how to come up with the percentages' or 'what are the breakeven probabilities', but this becomes quite advanced. There are many published documents that explain these in further detail with more critical intricacies. As stated, many major decisions are made with this concept.

4.04   Careful of Decision Bias

Finally, there is one last item when making decisions. Remember that we are human and emotions also play a factor when making decisions. This does not mean the decision will be better, even though it may feel better. For example, giving in to a child's tantrum may feel like the right decision to make at the time, but may not be the best decision for the long term as the child knows to have a tantrum to get their way. When possible, try to make the rational decision even when it may seem difficult emotionally.

There are many personal and emotional biases that do get in the way of the practical decision. I am not saying that this is always wrong, but you should know that these exist and be aware if you are making a decision based on your own personal bias or experience. The decision tree concept presented above is hopefully a way to get the emotion out of the decision so the decision is based on fact. You should be able to share and justify the decision tree to others, which will make you more confident with the final decision taken (especially with your family).

All decisions should include the relevant stakeholders and family members. When possible, it is important to make sure the people affected by the decision are part of it, which encourages buy-in. While there will always be a system for who will be responsible for making the ultimate decision, this encourages team members and families to acknowledge that one person's decisions are not isolated.

PART II

PRACTICAL LIFE ADVICE

Chapter 5 CODE OF CONDUCT

The next few topics are approached by many in different ways. I have tried to stay generic and logical. Everyone has their own approach on how to handle these topics for themselves. These are important 'other' topics (non-financial) that can also add to quality of life.

5.01   Being on Time

Time is one item I get criticized for because I arrive on time and insist others should do the same regardless of where they go. Unfortunately, not everybody accepts this view - it is acceptable to be fashionably late. However, there is no standard on 'fashionably'. In fact, in some countries, this could mean 60-90 minutes later. This is frustrating for both the host, who waits ready and has food prepared, and for those others who arrive on time.

Everybody hates waiting, so why do people make others wait for them? Furthermore, the time to meet was mutually agreed, so the late person has essentially broken a commitment, which is not a good character trait. Being habitually late is rude and not acceptable and there is no justified excuse for normally being late. Why do people not respect other's time?

Everyone can be on time – they choose not to. I have heard many people say "It's tough for us to get there on time. We have too much going on with kids, work, home, etc." But these same people can always be on time (if not early) for items they find important – picking up their kids, a movie, a flight, meeting with their boss, important clients, etc. So, everyone can be on time if they want – it just requires better planning.

I realize there may be a family emergency, road disaster, or some other unique circumstance that could cause you to be late. But this should be the exception and happen rarely, not the rule. A person who is habitually late (with or without an excuse) does not manage their own time well.

Time is the only fixed commodity we have. You cannot make more, save it for later use, or make it go faster or slower. It is the one constant that is always there. So why should we not respect this for everyone? Everyone's time is important, including our own. Not respecting another person's time means not respecting the person.

5.02   Children

I include this topic not because I am an expert on raising children. I don't believe anyone is. All kids are cute, fun, difficult, joyous, stressful, rewarding, etc. at different times as they grow. Each child is unique and will have different needs at varying times. But the items mentioned below worked for us, which is why I share them.

First, I am a big believer in 'nurture vs nature'. Kids may be born with physical traits, but not with their personality traits; they are raised to become that way. We are all creatures of the environment, situations, and values that have been presented to us or that we experienced. Children need to see good examples in their family and friends to emulate good values. School systems provide education, but learning and molding is never ending from everything that we are exposed to, especially in the first decade of our life.

When to have children:
- Be physically ready: This includes the usual first year of high physical stress and sleepless nights along with the following

years of running around after them. All is rewarding but requires effort and energy.

- Be mentally ready: Don't have kids due to 'society pressure' or 'why not now' mentality. You must be able and willing to change your life priorities to fully take care of another person. Also, as children get older, the physical stress changes to mental stress.
- Be financially ready: Yes, there will be extra costs along with a possible loss of income for one spouse. Be willing to give up some luxuries for the betterment of the family. Or, better yet, you should plan the added expense in your cashflow (as explained in Chapter 2).

Some parental rules of thumb to keep in mind:
- Establish the appropriate chain of command if there are disagreements. This does not mean the same person always has the final say. Divide the tasks and decide who the best person is to have the final say with regards to finances, house matters, external matters, etc. Hopefully, you can discuss and agree. If not, have a way to find a solution.
- Parents should keep a united front.
  - Do not allow kids to play one parent off the other. A child should not feel that they can get away with more from one parent.
  - Do not disagree with each other in front of kids, especially during discipline. You can argue later, but not in front of kids. There were many times where my wife or I did not agree with the decision the other made. But we supported it in front of the children and argued later.
  - Never make false threats as kids will learn not to take threats seriously. For example, "If you do that again, I'll

break your leg" is a false threat. If you make a threat, be able to follow through with it. This works especially well during tantrums if kids know their boundaries and realize the consequences are real.

- Make decisions *with* your children, not *for* them. Everybody likes to believe they have control, even kids. So, involve them in the decision – but you can control the options. For example, instead of saying "Take a bath", offer the option of "Would you rather take a bath or shower?"

- Think through the benefit of allowances, curfews, grounding, etc. Make sure these teach budgeting and build the long-term trust you want. We did not use any of these with our kids. While we always provided for their needs, we had our kids justify, earn, and/or demonstrate a valid need for when they wanted something. In some cases, I had them build a simple decision tree. In return, they appreciated the value in being part of the decision process.

- Obviously, physical abuse as a punishment is not acceptable. But kids need to know that consequences exist and will be enforced. So, a 'punishment' should be found that will affect the child. I believe that finding an item or privilege that the child cherishes and taking it away when needed normally works.

- Decisions and actions taken with the mind are always better than decisions taken with emotion. Think through the proper course of action, don't act out of anger.

- Have family meetings regularly to determine family priorities. Parents are the board and kids are shareholders. No one person should always be the priority as situations change. If all are involved, the more likely the family unit will succeed *together*.

- Have a clear list of priorities for your kids to follow. For example: 1) Safety, 2) Health, 3) Basic needs, 4) Future, 5) Long-term happiness, 6) Their wants. Be careful not to sacrifice a higher priority for a lower one.

5.03   Work Life Balance

Work-life balance is a topic that has (rightfully) gained momentum over the past few years. Achieving a good work-life balance can be challenging. Unfortunately, there is no one right answer for everyone as each person has different priorities. However, by not having a good balance, something will suffer - be it health, family, or some other item in *your* life which is important to *you*.

Balance in this case does not mean that all sides are equal. It means that you are allocating the appropriate time and effort to what you want. Time is the only constant we have – all of us get the same 60 minutes/hour, 24 hours/day, etc. No one gets more or less, you cannot bottle time to use it later, and you cannot bring back wasted time. Therefore, the better your time management, the higher chance you have to meet your goals.

<u>Work vs. Personal Time</u>
This used to be a clear solid line with the previous 8am-5pm schedule. But now remote work, mobility, flexible hours, etc. have made this a gray area with no specific boundaries. Priding yourself to work long hours may not always be the best decision, especially if it causes you to sacrifice a higher personal priority. So, to manage this, you need to make a personal agenda to set your boundaries and time blocks in advance, then stick to it.

Own vs. Family Time
Your personal time also gets split further between your own time (private time for yourself) and family time (loved ones in your life). Again, you need to figure out a good balance here. Many spend all their time on work and family. They forget about themselves which leads to personal health or mental issues. Otherwise, their time is spent on work and themselves which leads to separation from loved ones. Obviously, each person needs to decide the balance that works for them.

Technology and gadgets
We have all become slaves to our electronic gadgets in some form. How many times have you heard, or said it yourself, 'I can't live without my mobile.' One of my biggest frustrations is when people use their mobile when watching a movie in the theatre. Can they not switch off their device to enjoy the show they paid money to watch?

I remember a conversation I once had with a friend:
> Friend: *I never get time to relax. I get calls all day, into the evening, and sometime at night.*
> Me: *Have you thought about turning your phone off to get some peace and time for yourself?*
> Friend: *I could never do that. What if I miss an important call?*

Hence, the downward spiral continues and my friend was always tired. We live in fear thinking that by not being always available, the world might collapse without us. It's amazing that when we are feeling fine and energetic, we believe we are indispensable and should be contacted for everything. Yet, it's OK to be unreachable if you are ill or down with the flu. The logic does not fit. No one is that important that they can't have a couple hours to themselves whenever they need it.

You should find your own power-down time. It will improve you by making you more refreshed and relaxed, allowing you to concentrate on other items clearly.

Being out of balance
None of us are perfect and all will go through different cycles in life. Sometimes, the balance is working and sometimes it is not. When it is not, we further compound the problem by not listening to the warning signs.
- Running out of energy earlier in the day
- Health issues become worse and new issues develop
- Staying up late more often to accomplish tasks
- Friends, colleagues, or family members saying you need a break or you are not looking well

Take notice of the signs and listen to others (and your body) before the small problem becomes a big one. You will definitely benefit yourself and your family in the long run and help you get what you want out of life by taking control of the items in it.

5.04   Life Rules & Principles

This section is included because it worked for my family and my kids (all adults) still live by them today. As our kids were growing, we thought it best to come up with simple rules that the kids could remember and follow and use at different phases of their life. Surprisingly, these stuck with them and benefitted everyone, especially them. The ages identified in parentheses are the ages I suggest implementing the rules – but every parent knows their child better.

- Standard Rules (approx. age 3-9): When the family would go for an outing (a picnic or amusement park or mall), we sat the kids down and told them to always follow three simple rules – listen (to each other and us), stay together, and have fun. What's funny is that when someone did not follow these rules, one of the kids complained to us. So, although unexpected, the rules seemed to work. After a while, we did not need to specify the rules, we just had to say 'Standard Rules.' Later, the kids would even say "Dad – we know" which was great.

- Decision Making (approx. age 10-high school): As the kids grew older, they start going out on their own. We cannot watch them all the time. The thought of peer pressure and experimentation became a concern. With the success of Standard Rules, what advice could we give them to make the right decision in a situation? So, we came up with these three decision-making thoughts and told our kids to ask themselves these questions before agreeing to do something:

    - Is it legal? – Is what you are doing or asked to do legal?
    - Can I tell my parents or friends? (i.e. people I feel accountable to) – Am I comfortable going home and telling my parents or friend what I did?
    - Voice inside? – Does that little voice (or conscience) inside you support your decision?

    If you can justify the answers to the above, you are probably okay taking the decision and we will support you.

- Going Out (high school onwards): To avoid being caught somewhere without a way out, the advice became a little more mature.

- Personal Safety – this is first and foremost important. Always be observant of your surroundings. Don't get caught in a situation where you forget what's around you.
- Have a friend/partner – don't go alone. This is more in case you get hurt, not sure about something, but obviously there are other benefits. If going out drinking, have you agreed the designated sober person you can trust?
- Trapped in a corner – when at a public place or friend's party, make sure you have a simple clear path to an exit. When in a group, don't get trapped in a corner or basement where it will be difficult for you to get out.
- Contingency plan home – if your main way of getting home fails, what is your backup? Your ride may go home early, public transport may not run, etc. If I (parent) am the backup, then you agree to tell me your movements so I know where to come if needed.

- Life priorities (lifetime): During your life, always remember the following life priorities AND in this order:
  - 1. Health – Always take care of your health first. Without this, you will not enjoy anything else.
  - 2. Family – Remember that family is important and we are here for you. Don't forget to keep all members involved in your life.
  - 3. Job/Education – If in school, then education is third priority. If working, then job/career is third priority.

  Never sacrifice a higher priority item for a lower priority unless you have carefully thought it through. You will not enjoy the lower priority items if you don't take care of the higher ones.

Even companies encourage employees to follow the same priorities as it is in the company's best interest to increase retention and employee satisfaction.

Finally, in summary, remember the three key items that bring stability in life: relationships, house, job. Always keep these core items of life in order.

5.05　What Are Your Personal Values

We all have values – some we practice more than others. What is important about values is to have resilience (be true to your values) and integrity (be consistent and adhere to your values). There are many different values that one follows. Some examples of commonly held values:

- Truthfulness – honesty, keeping promises, communicating clearly and accurately, veracity, trustworthiness
- Love/Compassion – helping and caring for others, putting others needs before your own
- Fairness – equality, symmetry, treating others as you'd want to be treated, respect for life
- Freedom – of expression and action, from oppression, open-mindedness
- Unity – inclusiveness, community, cooperation, consensus
- Tolerance – acknowledging dignity of all, respecting rights of others, refusing to hate, being open to other points of view
- Accountability – for yourself, your feelings, behaviors, your future
- Courage – to speak the truth, perseverance, diligence, integrity, genuineness
- Temperance – self-control, prudence, discretion, humility, and modesty

- Transcendence – gratitude, optimism, forgiveness, playfulness, passion

While we all like to consider ourselves perfect, no one can adhere to all the values all the time (need to be realistic). But it is important to find the few that represent who you are. Once you have identified the two or three that are core to you, know them and actively practice them when dealing with others. The goal is when someone thinks of you, you want to be known by your core values. This can only be done by demonstrating them consistently.

5.06   Other Tips

Finally, the next set of items are tidbits that worked for many. They are simple pieces of advice that make life easier, especially in the working world. Use these at your discretion:

- When you want something done, never ask a question that requires a yes/no answer. It is always easy for the other person to say 'no'. Ask open-ended questions.
- At your job, keep your assistant/secretary, your boss's secretary, and the Tech Support person happy – it will make your own work life easier.
- Sometimes, in a company, forgiveness is easier than permission. Have your audit trail to show why your decision was better for the company and why you made it.
- Get what someone wants you to do in writing (or email) when you can. If genuine, the person will gladly do it and provides legitimacy to the request.
- Be ready to ride the coat tails of someone moving up. Hard work may also get you there, but why not take every

opportunity you can. Note, I am not saying to break any rules or policies. But, if someone can pull you up with them, no harm in taking the helping hand.

- There are three kinds of people in this world. Those that learn from others' mistakes, those that learn from their own mistakes, those that never learn. We all hope we are part of the first group – but only a few are. Most are part of the second group and there are some who are, unfortunately, part of the third group.

Chapter 6 SENSITIVE TOPICS

The next few topics are sensitive in nature as everyone has their own views of how they choose to handle it for themselves. Hence, I accept that my values and beliefs may be different to yours, which is fine. I include these topics as a trigger so that you and your family can have the discussion together.

6.01 Importance of Health

This is one we hear about all the time, but it cannot be stressed enough. As mentioned earlier, always take care of your health first and make it your highest priority. Without this, you will not enjoy anything else. This is one of my regrets in life – like most of us, I could (and should) have done a better job.

It's funny that we take better care of our cars than we do our bodies. We take our cars for routine maintenance and check-ups, get the mechanic to fix all the little noises, and do whatever we can so the car will last us the longest. But how many of us go in for an annual medical exam or blood test? Why do we not see a doctor for minor pains or when our bodies are not functioning optimally? We wait until a problem becomes serious, which sometimes is too late.

Unfortunately, the human body is very resilient which gives us a false sense of security. The human heart is the world's best machine – continuously pumping non-stop from the day we are born to the day we die. In our early years, we are busy learning about the world. In our teens, we are finding ourselves. In our twenties, we believe we are indestructible (survive on too much or too little sleep, food, exercise, work). Our body stays fine. In our thirties, we get tied down with family and work commitments. In our forties, the body starts to push back. You now realize that you have another 40+ years to live and the body also needs care (and you hope it is not too late).

As the world has started to live longer, you see an attitude difference in thinking and physical health in elderly people. Before, when life spans were around 65 (plus or minus), most people had mentally 'lived their life', hence passed. But their physical health was still decent. Today, people can and want to live much longer. But they have not taken care of their body to last for the 80-90 years desired.

I had a friend who wanted to start an exercise routine. But he felt stuck.
> Friend: *I want to work out at least three times a week but just can't find the time.*
> Me: *OK. So why don't you start by working out once a week?*
> Friend: *What good would that do?*

Human nature is fascinating. It's easier to dream about exercising three times a week rather than actually exercising once a week. Investing time in our health will also pay good returns. As stated earlier for investing money, the same applies to exercising: don't overextend yourself – start small but start!

There is no guarantee to being healthy. But instead of having aspirations to become healthy, take positive action to make it happen. We should all take better decisions early to allow us the opportunity to stay healthy for the long term.

6.02   How Does Religion Fit

This is an interesting (and sensitive) topic which has become risky to talk about. However, it is important as it is a key part of many cultures and shapes our thinking. I am not here to promote any specific religion, but mainly to open the door and encourage everyone to have discussions about it.

I was raised in a Hindu house in a Christian society. Everywhere I lived (USA, Europe, Asia, Middle East), I tried to talk about religion with others to learn and understand their views and appreciate the differences. It is very interesting and educational to learn about different beliefs from those who are willing to discuss it rationally. I have been to churches, mosques, temples, etc. as I respect all faiths. While one person may not agree with another's religious views (which is okay), understanding it helps bridge the difference of opinion, actions, and relationships.

I have found that all religions are based on the same fundamentals: don't lie or cheat, treat others properly, don't steal, be faithful, etc. However, the difference is how religion is practiced and preached. All religions are based on belief, which is why they are difficult to argue. You cannot argue beliefs – you can only argue facts, science, and logic which do not exist in religion. Religions are based on the views, beliefs, and interpretations which have been passed down from holy books and religious scholars for many generations. Religions, traditions, superstitions, and cultures all have one thing in common – they are all based on how we were raised. For those with strong beliefs, there is no logical rationale that can change their view.

Religion is great in that it provides inner peace and guidance for many people. The problem occurs when we start forcing our religion and beliefs on others. No one religion is the best, always right, or followed in its entirety. Deviations occur because the situation requires it. I have come across many who follow their religion selectively (when it suits them) and hide behind it when they want - or don't want - to do something. This further complicates the understanding which then questions the true meaning.

Our younger generation is becoming more global and questioning many beliefs. As such, views on what is right or traditional are also changing and are situation specific. Global views (societal and legal) on marriage, divorce, LGBT, single parenting, surrogacy, etc. are constantly debated, changed, and accepted. So, religions should also allow flexibility, or else they will not be followed at all.

I have often been asked about my personal religion and views. Because of huge religious contradictions I have seen in my life, I became what is known as 'Agnostic' – I believe in the concept of God (higher being), but not in religion. I believe there is a Supreme being, a Creator – does not matter the name given (as different religions choose to do). The reason I believe in God is that there are so many things in this world that cannot be explained through conventional wisdom. God is the ultimate judge for all of us and will make the decision based on how we live our life. I do my best to practice the basic fundamentals that (I believe) are in all religions – do good for others, live an honest life, have integrity, value relationships, take care of family, etc. I am not perfect – no one is. But I choose to believe in living via good virtues and not religious rituals. I think this is what God intends and wants. Again, this is my personal belief.

There is a Bollywood move called "*PK*" (it's a Hindi movie but can be found with English subtitles). It is one of my favorite movies because it addresses the differences and contradictions that occur in religion. All religions believe in a God or some type of supreme being. The message "*PK*" gives is that if all religions believe in one God, why are there so many different (sometimes conflicting) rituals to please the same supreme being. If God is all-forgiving and fair to all, then God is not discriminatory in what someone chooses to follow, and that person should not be judged because of it or punished for believing differently.

Ritual followers should be 'God loving people', not 'God fearing people'. Religious rituals should be followed because we believe it in our heart – not because society requires it or we believe we will be punished if we don't. It should bring happiness, contentment, and inner peace. This is the guidance we should pass on to the next generation. I feel our future educated and diverse generations, who access worldwide internet information and cultures, will have a difficult time blindly following a faith that does not fit in today's global society.

6.03   Death & Wills

Death is a sensitive topic in itself – many are uncomfortable discussing mortality when there is no 'imminent' reason to do so. But we should talk more openly about death. It is a fact of life – it is not a question of 'if', but 'when'. We have all gone through the loss of a family member, loved one, or close friend. While I wish a long life to all and it is what we all want and hope for, it is not uncommon to lose someone in an unexpected and/or very sudden manner. And then, after having dealt with grieving and funeral arrangements, there is nothing worse for those that survive than having to deal with estate affairs of the deceased without any guidance or plan to what the deceased wanted.

I personally think this is unfair to do to my family, or anyone left behind. They should be comfortable, capable, and willing to carry out whatever is required. So, why not be prepared in advance. Now, if you are someone who 'believes' talking about something will make it happen, then this discussion may not be for you.

I remember a discussion with my dad when I was in middle school. Friends at school started talking about inheritance. So, I mustered the courage to ask my dad "Will I get any inheritance?" My dad gave me an answer I still remember to this day. He said, "If you are smart, you won't need it and if you are stupid, I don't want to give it to you. So, don't expect anything." Now, as harsh as this sounds, there is a lot of truth in it and it was difficult to argue back. It also solidified the need that I should be able to stand on my own.

While growing up, our family was very open about discussing death and wills. I think I was fourteen when my dad first had this discussion with me. Also, due to the different laws in different states of the USA, it was important to my parents that local legal issues were understood.

It is important to have a Last Will & Testament. In fact, in addition to the will, one should also make a future cashflow (explained in section 2.03) both with and without the main earner. The family can then see how cashflow needs can change when an unexpected death happens.

In some parts of the world, the estate division is pre-decided by religion (e.g. Sharia law), acceptable culture norms, or by the government. But this still does not mean the discussion with the family cannot happen. The more discussion a family has on the topic, the less scary the end of life will become for all concerned.

Chapter 7 WHAT SCHOOLS DON'T TEACH

As far as I know, cashflow and money management is not formally taught in most school systems, even though it is the most fundamental item that is required to be successful in any field. I have given courses at many different work locations and, more recently, gave a short discussion to a high school graduating class. Surprisingly, when I talked to the kids, other adults and parents would come and say, "I wish someone taught me those things earlier in life."

So, this chapter is really for students – essentially high school students going off to college and college students who will soon be responsible for their own financial future. While the basic principles are no different, a student's money issues are more about managing spending – not future cash growth.

As parents, we send our kids off to college to learn a specialty which will allow them to make a future on their own. Colleges are great at providing the foundation for a specific career. But as parents/guardians, it is our responsibility to also teach our kids about financial discipline once they leave home as the college will not teach them that.

I always hear parents say "My child spends too much money at college, always asking for more." I then ask, "Do you or your child know where the money is going?" Normally, the answer is "No". Obviously, if you don't know where the money is going, then how do you know if it is too little, too much, what is being wasted, or what can be improved for the future. As explained in previous chapters, this is because most adults don't know where their own money is going - so how can they expect their children to know?

We should all be held accountable for our actions and financial decisions.

So, below are some tips and advice to share with your student about money:

- Make kids accountable for their spending. They should track their funds and be able to justify back to parents the money they spent (where and why). Just because parents cover all costs does not mean it should be unlimited. This not only builds trust between parent and student but also helps the student realize the value of tracking. Yes, it will take extra time for both of you, but will be worth it.

- If possible, avoid cash and use a debit or campus card. This will make it easier to track. If using cash, keep a detailed list of where the cash is spent.

- Before going out with friends, be aware of how the bill will be settled – split evenly, each pay for what is ordered, other options. It is better to agree in advance if possible. This also applies with roommates, drinks, parties.

- Gourmet cafe costs (i.e. Starbucks, Costa, etc.) add up. This is not to say eliminate them completely. But realize they are a luxury, not a necessity.

- Eating out and ordering in is easy, but also adds up. Remember you may have a pre-paid meal plan.

- A car is normally not needed while attending college. The parking hassles, insurance costs, and maintenance issues all deter from keeping a car. Taxi options (such as Uber) are good for backup, but should not be taken for granted. There are other options to consider such as the metro, bus, or other ride sharing options.

- Loans and credit cards are easily offered to college students. After all, banks want to earn interest. Having debt is not bad provided you know how to manage it. If poorly handled, it can result in a bad credit rating which will affect the student in the long term. So, it is important to realize how to handle these enticements.

There are many methods that can be used to track spending – spreadsheets, phone apps, bank statements offer breakdown, etc. Use whatever method works for you and has the categories you want to manage. I personally believe spreadsheets are the best and easiest to customize.

The next couple pages are examples from my kids' college days.

Spreadsheet entries

DATE	CODE	PAYMENT	DEPOSIT	BALANCE	TO/FROM WHO
12.11	PHONE	$155.21		$7,015.63	Phone
12.12	EATOUT	$6.96		$7,008.67	Subway
12.11	EATOUT	$1.35		$7,007.32	Food
12.12	FAMILY	$26.44		$6,980.88	Drinks
12.13	FAMILY	$14.99		$6,965.89	Prime Fresh
12.10	EATOUT	$52.14		$6,913.75	Restaurant
12.12	EATOUT	$7.65		$6,906.10	Uptowner
12.13	TRAV	$41.67		$6,864.43	Uber
12.15	APT	$119.38		$6,745.05	Internet
12.22	APT	$11.99		$6,733.06	TV
12.27	DEP		$2,000.00	$8,733.06	Money from Dad
11.14	EATOUT	$34.78		$8,698.28	Restaurant
1.03	LEISURE	$21.19		$8,677.09	Games
1.06	GROC	$39.84		$8,637.25	Whole Foods
1.14	LEISURE	$21.19		$8,616.06	Games
1.19	PHONE	$49.91		$8,566.15	Phone charger
1.02	APT	$81.91		$8,484.24	Utilities
1.03	APT	$4,366.36		$4,117.88	January rent
1.07	GROC	$2.99		$4,114.89	Whole Foods
1.08	GROC	$15.16		$4,099.73	Pasta sides
1.07	TRAV	$40.69		$4,059.04	Uber
1.08	SCHOOL	$168.54		$3,890.50	Textbooks

Family as a Business

Monthly Summary

	Month1	Month2	Month3	Month4	Month5	Month6	TOTAL
BEG. BAL.	0	1,231	1,970	4,107	664	(2,374)	
DEP	4,000	4,025	7,896	5,000	6,118	3,000	$30,038
CASH	0	(20)	0	(23)	0	0	($43)
GROC	(378)	(249)	(5)	(299)	(338)	(99)	($1,368)
EATOUT	(692)	(405)	(207)	(162)	(228)	(236)	($1,930)
SCHOOL	(654)	26	(64)	(437)	0	0	($1,129)
FAMILY	(366)	0	(69)	0	(121)	(251)	($808)
TRAV	0	(321)	(429)	(173)	(46)	(246)	($1,215)
APT	(156)	(183)	(4681)	(4587)	(7663)	895	($16,374)
ONLINE	0	0	0	0	0	0	$0
LEISURE	(152)	(52)	0	(56)	(106)	(50)	($417)
HEALTH	0	(1,626)	0	(2,447)	0	0	($4,073)
MISC	(54)	(174)	0	(15)	(405)	(27)	($675)
SHOP	(43)	0	(100)	(3)	104	0	($43)
CAB	(224)	(58)	0	(28)	(68)	(35)	($414)
METRO	0	0	0	0	(10)	0	($10)
PHONE	(50)	(223)	(205)	(213)	(273)	(192)	($1,156)
	1,231	1,970	4,107	664	(2,374)	385	

DEP	= MONEY IN
CASH	= ATM WITHDRAWALS
GROC	= GROC (FOOD/TOILETRIES ETC.)
EATOUT	= GROC OFF CAMPUS (EATING OUT)
SCHOOL	= SUPPLIES/BOOKS/TUITION/
FAMILY	= VISITS/ONLINE PURCHASES
TRAV	= TRAVEL ACTIVITIES
APT	= APT SUPPLIES AND COSTS (UTILITY, CABLE, NON-GROCERY ITEMS)
ONLINE	= ONLINE PURCHASES/PAYMENTS (PERSONAL)
LEISURE	= ENTERTAINMENT/WEEKEND ACTIVITIES
HEALTH	= ANYTHING DEALING WITH HEALTH
MISC	= ITEMS WHICH COULD NOT BE CLASSIFIED UNDER ANYTHING ELSE
SHOP	= SHOPPING (PERSONAL)
CAB	= CAB RIDES (UBER)
METRO	= METRO COSTS
PHONE	= IPHONE, CALLS, ETC.

What Schools Don't Teach

When my kids came home during their semester break, we would go through their summary to see if all was in line or anything should be changed. The kids would need to justify where the money they received went. After reviewing their spreadsheet, we could identify if, how, or where improvements should be made. The added benefit is that my kids still use this philosophy to track their own expenditures even though they have graduated college.

Final plea: If you are not able to properly educate your student on financial matters, please (please! please!) have them take a course or seminar on budgeting and discounting to learn the time value of money. They then can make better investment decisions once they have their own money.

Chapter 8 QUOTES

These quotes were noted from different sources throughout my life: church boards, motivational slogans, historical speeches, billboards, posters, etc. I am sure they have made the rounds in different versions and formats over many decades. This is a simple compilation of ones that resonated with me. Although it is impossible to remember all of them, try to take a few, remember those, and then live by them. My primary one was the first one, although I reviewed the list routinely to keep in mind important values.

1. Never get so busy making a living that you forget to make a life.

2. We make a living by what we get. We make a life by what we give.

3. If you fail to control the events in your life, then events in your life will control you.

4. Blaming your faults on your nature does not change the nature of your faults.

5. Until you value yourself, you will not value your time. Until you value your time, you will not do anything with it. Time cannot be managed or controlled, but events can. Time will continue to go on whether or not we manage it.

6. Wisdom is knowing what to do next, skill is knowing how to do it, and virtue is doing it.

7. Life is like riding a bicycle. You don't fall off unless you stop pedaling and you must keep moving to maintain balance.

8. Everyone is trying to accomplish something big not realizing that life is made up of little things.

9. Most good judgment comes from experience. Most experience comes from bad judgments.

10. Our eyes are placed in front because it is more important to look ahead than to look back.

11. It's better to let someone think you are an idiot than to open your mouth and prove it.

12. If you blame others for your failures, do you credit them for your achievements?

13. Success isn't the key to happiness – Happiness is the key to success.

14. You may be only one person in the world, but you may also be the world to one person.

15. God gives you blessings, happiness is up to you.

16. People ask for many things to enjoy life, they forget they have been given life to enjoy many things.

17. The mind is like a parachute – it doesn't work unless it is open.

18. There is a huge difference between growing older and growing up. Growing old is mandatory, growing up is optional.

19. Real people don't love the most beautiful person in the world. They love the person who can make their world the most beautiful.

20. People are made to be loved and things are made to be used. The confusion in this world is that people are used and things are loved.

21. Pain is inevitable, suffering is optional.

22. Success is getting what you want. Happiness is wanting what you get.

23. Don't measure activity. Measure accomplishments. It's not how busy you are that counts, but whether the output is greater than inputs.

24. If a ship captain's primary job was to protect his ship and crew, he would never leave the shore. But that's not the purpose of a ship. New experiences are only realized when you get out of your comfort zone.

25. Every day may not be good…but there's something good in every day.

26. You don't have to be great to get started, but you have to get started to be great.

Chapter 9 CLOSING REMARKS

I hope this book gets you started to make a better future for your family. Once you start, you will realize there is a great benefit for you to follow the lessons presented. And, after you start, it will be easier to keep all your information current and up to date.

There will be many hurdles in life. How high the hurdles are will depend on how well prepared a person is to tackle them. Along those lines, we have to be very careful in choosing our pursuits, because our habits make us. Cultivating good habits that follow below will send you in the right direction. They'll help you to lead a more meaningful and fulfilling life, whereby you cultivate the best within yourself.

- Stay away from people who erode your quality of life. Life is good and it is up to you to see it that way.
- Realize that things aren't always as you perceive them to be. Dig deeper to find the true issues.
- In any endeavor, get started, even though you might fail. You will never succeed without trying, but without trying you have already failed.
- Get organized. More important – stay organized.
- Start a collection of the things that truly resonate with you.
- Do something that reminds you of who you are and what you enjoy.
- Say 'no' firmly when you <u>need</u> to – don't always be nice.
- Stick to realistic goals – a goal without a plan is only a wish.

Your character is determined by your attitude and how you spend your time, and so is happiness. Stop chasing the things that you think might make you happy in the future and start realizing that your peace and happiness are now and are entirely up to you. As anywhere in life or work, it is important to laugh and keep a smile on your face.

There are three mindsets of people in the world:
- Those that live in the past. They use statements such as 'Life used to be good when…(kids were home, things were simpler, I was in college, etc.)'
- Those that live in the future. They use statements such as 'Life will be good when…(I get that raise/promotion, we buy a bigger house, I lose weight, etc.)'
- Those that live in the present. Those that realize that life is good now. These people are the happiest.

It does not mean the past and future are not important – one should remember the past, plan for the future, but live in the present.

While trying to pursue happiness, people like using many excuses when things are not going their way. I have listed here three excuses that I commonly hear and why they are not valid:
- Excuse #1: "I don't have time". We have heard this from others and perhaps said it ourselves. But this is a poor excuse. Everyone has 24 hours/day, 7 days/week, 12 months/year, etc. No one has more or less. The goal is managing time and not letting time control you. For the important things in life, you find time or make time. People have time to send multiple emails, post on social media, watch TV, etc. So, not making time for your own future is not making your future a priority.
- Excuse #2: "That might work for YOU, but not for me". How do you know without trying? Sure, we are all different, but find the key elements that made it work and implement those.

- Excuse #3: "I don't want to look bad and fail". I guarantee there will be ideas that fail. But this does not mean you don't try – you just proceed cautiously. I'm sure those with kids tell them this same philosophy. Always think, "Will what I'm doing get me where I want to be in the future".

I wish you the best and hope this book gets you to where you want for a long and happy successful life for you and your family.

www.ingramcontent.com/pod-product-compliance
Lightning Source LLC
Chambersburg PA
CBHW031446210526
45464CB00005B/2343